Hydroponics

The complete guide to horticulture without soil; Learn how to quickly grow organic vegetables, herbs, and fruits. Easy DIY

Table Of Contents

Chapter One: Introduction

Hydroponic System

THIS BOOK MAKES HYDROPONICS ACCESSIBLE to garden workers of any experience level. You'll learn both the study of hydroponics and its pragmatic applications and see that DIY hydroponics isn't only an approach to abstain from buying costly hydroponic system s; it's likewise an approach to make a lovely garden more qualified to your requirements. Offering assemble guides for hydroponic gardens that run from easy to complex, this book shows systems appropriate for almost any environment or application. The assemble guides incorporate numerous choices for modifying the plan so you can make a garden obliged your space, crop determination, and spending plan. Furthermore, this book offers important seed assortment proposals that can spare new hydroponic plant specialists time and cash that could have effortlessly been squandered on ineffectively fit harvest determinations. Gain from Farmer Tyler's tremendous experience and evade the expensive mix-ups normally made by new hydroponic producers. The more you know, the better you develop!

WHAT IS HYDROPONICS?

Set forth plainly, hydroponics is developing plants without soil. The vast majority accept that dirt is irreplaceable for plant development, yet if you have this book, you likely definitely realize that isn't so. The different elements of soil can be reproduced utilizing different materials. Soil offers help for the plant since it makes a physical structure for the roots to get a handle on. Tall trees would be not able to hold themselves upstanding on a breezy day without a firm grasp in the dirt. In a hydroponic system, the physical help furnished by soil can be recreated with an assortment of materials and trellis structures.

Soil likewise gives basic Nutrients to plant development. These equivalent Nutrients can be provided utilizing elective techniques, be that as it may. Hydroponic system s apportion water-dissolvable Nutrients got from both natural and regular sources. Soil can likewise give a home to fundamental microbial populaces that make valuable associations with plant roots. These equivalent microorganisms can live and flourish in a hydroponic domain. Things being what they are, if hydroponics is basically reproducing the job of soil, why not simply use soil?

History of Hydroponics

Hydroponics was drilled numerous hundreds of years back in Amazon, Babylon, Egypt, china and India where old men utilized broke up fertilizer to develop cucumber, watermelons and different vegetables in sandy riverbeds. The "hanging solidify of Babylon" and the Aztec's skimming ranches were really models of hydroponic system s. Afterward, when plant physiologists began to develop plants with explicit Nutrients for exploratory purposes, they gave the name "nutriculture."

Enthusiasm for down to earth use of "nutriculture" created in 1925 when the green house industry communicated enthusiasm for its utilization. Green house soils must be supplanted oftentimes to defeat issues of soil structure, ripeness and vermin. Therefore, scientists got intrigued by the potential utilization of nutriculture to supplant ordinary soil culture.

In 1929, Dr. William F. Gericke of the University of California prevailing with regards to developing tomato vines of 7.5 m stature in supplement arrangements. He named this new creation system "hydroponics" a word got from Greek to mirror the significance of 'Hydros' (water) and 'Ponos' (working). Along these lines, hydroponics broke the research center limits and entered the universe of pragmatic cultivation. The term hydroponics initially implied supplement arrangement culture. Be that as it may, crop developing in latent strong media utilizing supplement arrangement is additionally remembered for hydroponics in expansive sense.

During 1960s and 70s, business hydroponics ranches were created in Abu Dhabi, Arizona, Belgium, California, Denmark, German, Holland, Iran, Italy, Japan, Russian Federation and different nations. During 1980s, many robotized and modernized hydroponics ranches were set up far and wide. Home hydroponics units got well known during 1990s.

Chapter Two: Advantages And Disadvantages Components

Preferences OF HYDROPONIC GROWING

1. Doesn't require quality soil

Cultivating is regularly thought of as a movement restricted to those blessed enough to have a garden. Hydroponics significantly builds planting alternatives for those in homes without gardens or those with yards that have soil ineffectively appropriate for consumable yields.

Hydroponics joined with indoor developing systems gives cultivators much more choices by extending the potential garden space to almost any place in the home.

2. Potential for quicker harvest development

Plants infrequently augment their full development potential in soil. There is quite often some restricting component hindering their development. In soil, the plant pulls need to look for Nutrients that are frequently unevenly appropriated and potentially blocked off in light of the fact that they are bound to different soil particles. A few Nutrients are unavailable in light of the fact that the organisms in the dirt presently can't seem to separate the supplement hotspot (for instance, excrement) into a structure that is accessible to the plant's foundations. It is additionally workable for the plant development to be compelled by an absence of water or an excessive amount of water. An excessive amount of water can lessen the measure of oxygen accessible to the roots and restrain natural procedures important for the roots to take-up Nutrients and water. Hydroponics washes the roots in an exact mix of fundamental Nutrients with an equalization of water and oxygen. A significant number of the requirements on a plant's potential development can be killed or diminished utilizing hydroponics and indoor developing systems.

3. Requires less space

A plant must spread its foundations far and wide during the time spent scanning for water and Nutrients. By dispensing with the requirement for the plant roots to discover water and Nutrients, the separating of plants is just constrained by the territory required for the plant overhang.

4. Less requirement on developing season

Clearly, developing inside licenses plant specialists to broaden the developing season. Less clearly, hydroponics explicitly can broaden the developing season in any event, when set outside. Frequently the temperature of a plant's foundations is more basic to its wellbeing than the leaf temperature. It is conceivable to develop winter crops in 100°F if the root temperature is kept in an ideal range nearer to 65° to 75°F. It is additionally conceivable to develop crops that lean toward warm temperatures in chilly atmospheres by expanding the root zone temperature. Hydroponics builds the capacity to unequivocally alter the root zone temperature. Through utilization of heater s, chillers, or straightforward practices like covering a hydroponic supply, a hydroponic garden worker can increment or abatement water temperature and improve crop development.

5. Can be utilized in any area

Hydroponics permits planters to develop in zones that don't have quality soil. Hydroponics additionally permits plant specialists to develop in areas that would be unsuited for crops because of unfriendly atmosphere or restricted water get to. Probably the greatest open door for hydroponics is developing in deserts. Deserts regularly have a Central atmosphere for developing harvests, with bunches of light and little vermin nearness, yet they are restricted in access to water. Hydroponics utilizes significantly less water than conventional techniques and can make cultivating in deserts a reasonable choice. Hydroponics is additionally the essential strategy used to develop plants in space. Numerous harvests, including lettuce, have been developed in space utilizing hydroponic strategies.

Leafy vegetables can be grown hydroponically in outer space. Photo courtesy of NASA.

6. Uses less water

Hydroponics utilizes less water since you may reuse any water system water not legitimately taken up by the harvest. In soil, a significant part of the water is lost to dissipation and waste. In hydroponics, vanishing can be decreased or disposed of by covering the water repository, and all waste water is gathered to be reused.

7. No weeding and no herbicides

No weeding. It might appear to be a little point from the start, yet after a period of pulling garden weeds, most customary soil plant specialists couldn't imagine anything better than to have invested that energy accomplishing something progressively fun, such as getting ready dishes from their reap. Hydroponic producers additionally have no compelling reason to buy herbicides.

Moreover, hydroponic producers never need to confront the potential harvest harm of herbicide float when a breeze incidentally blows herbicide onto your garden and harms or slaughters your valuable plants.

8. Can decrease or take out requirement for pesticides

Hydroponic gardens, particularly those outside and in gardens, are seldom bother free, however hydroponics has the possibility to decrease bug pressure. Hydroponic gardens present less concealing spots for bothers that will tunnel into soil or stow away in rotting plant flotsam and jetsam. At the point when hydroponics is joined with indoor developing strategies it is conceivable to have a totally bug free garden if the plant specialist rehearses preventive bug control procedures. Preventive vermin control systems are canvassed in the Equipment for Growing Indoors area of the Equipment section.

9. Can lessen or wipe out agrarian spillover

It is hard to oversee overflow in a conventional garden. The plant specialist may treat the garden and the following week a rainstorm washes away a significant part of the Nutrients. It is likewise conceivable that the Nutrients will be diverted by typical water system.

Utilizing progressed hydroponic methods it is conceivable to have zero spillover. This is a training most appropriate for proficient hydroponic cultivators as it includes propelled water testing, science, and a broad information on a yield's particular supplement necessities. For home hydroponic plant specialists, it is entirely expected to flush or dump out the supplement arrangement in the hydroponic system at regular intervals to maintain a strategic distance from potential supplement issue in the yield made by an awkwardness in Nutrients. Plants don't devour all Nutrients at a similar rate, so after some time some aggregate and some become lacking. Occasional flushes, or changes of the supplement arrangement, help reset the system and guarantee the yield approaches the right equalization of Nutrients. This wastewater doesn't need to be basically flushed down, however; most hydroponic cultivators utilize this water for their outside garden or pruned plants. A customary soil-based garden is an extraordinary ally to a hydroponic garden.

10. Ability to control supplement content

One of the most widely recognized misinterpretations encompassing hydroponics is that hydroponic produce has a lower supplement thickness than soil-developed produce in light of the fact that hydroponic yields are developed in water. There have been numerous investigations looking at the supplement thickness of hydroponic and soil-developed produce and the results are equally blended. There are such a large number of components that influence the supplement thickness of a yield, and in spite of the fact that manure plays a job wherein Nutrients are available, the earth has an enormous job wherein Nutrients the plant really takes-up.

Light power and explicit shades of light can influence cancer prevention agent content. Worry because of water system practices can influence cancer prevention agent content. Temperature can influence sugar focus. There is a not insignificant rundown of components that influence the Nutrients present in a harvest at the same time, by and large, these vegetables are nutritious. The distinctions are exact moment and it is hard to turn out badly when eating a vegetable. Almost all plants will give noticeable indications of supplement inadequacy if their supplement thickness is altogether off from typical levels, so if the plant looks great it more than likely will have a supplement profile tantamount to a comparative looking plant paying little mind to nature in which it was developed.

All things considered, there are some novel techniques that hydroponic cultivators are utilizing to control their yield. Numerous business hydroponic tomato cultivators intentionally stress their plants with high supplement levels at key stages in their advancement to prompt an expansion in sugar content in the tomatoes. The producers can spike the Nutrients to initiate the sugar increment and afterward diminish the Nutrients to a typical level to keep up solid development. For lettuce, the Oizumi Yasaikobo Co., Ltd., in Chichibu City, Japan, has built up a technique for developing low-potassium lettuce utilizing hydroponic strategies. The homestead develops these strength lettuces for clients experiencing kidney sickness who are getting treated with dialysis and are limited from expending vegetables with a high potassium content. This push to develop produce with a custom supplement content is one of numerous comparative tasks being created far and wide as cultivators gain the capacity to unequivocally control each part of a harvest's developing environment.

11. Increased capacity to coordinate harvest development for explicit attributes

Not exclusively would nutrient be able to content be controlled, yet different attributes, for example, leaf size, leaf shading, root size, and plant tallness, can likewise be controlled when hydroponics is joined with indoor developing. Indoor garden workers can utilize different shades of light to actuate explicit attributes. A mainstream practice is the utilization of blue light to develop progressively smaller plants inside to diminish the vertical space required for a yield.

12. Clean and low chaos

Soil cultivating can be muddled. This isn't awful, however not constantly perfect. The most extraordinary model is the International Space Station. A coasting haze of soil would be a calamity around that delicate gear. For those of us not developing plants in space, the advantage of soilless developing is a cleaner crop. Harvests developed hydroponically frequently require next to zero washing. Hydroponic gardens can be an incredible method to open children to plants in a study hall or home without acquiring the capability of a major sloppy wreckage. One of my preferred child cordial system s is the hydroponic pixie garden portrayed in the Media Beds segment of the Hydroponic Growing Systems part.

13. Can be simpler and less work than developing in soil

Simple to utilize fertilizers, simple to computerize, and no weeding are only a couple of the reasons hydroponic cultivating can be far easier than customary techniques. Hydroponics may appear to be scaring to novices, however after a harvest or two most hydroponic plant specialists are snared.

14. Easy to ace and recreate results

Hydroponic yields develop rapidly, permitting producers to get more involvement with a shorter timeframe. The best instructor is understanding, and more quickly developing yields permit hydroponic producers to adapt rapidly. When a cultivator makes sense of the correct formula for that environment and chose crop, it is anything but difficult to recreate the procedure. Hydroponics enables the producer to imitate the specific Nutrients accessible and water system recurrence. At the point when hydroponics is matched with indoor developing strategies, producers increment their control considerably further. Indoor plant specialists can recreate light power, light term, temperature, mugginess, carbon dioxide levels, and wind stream to develop steady yields all year without the regular and yearly variances experienced by conventional plant specialists.

15. Increases capacity to oversee soilborne pathogens like root decays and bacterial shrinks

Probably the most forceful plant pathogens are soilborne. Any producer who has struggled root spoil or bacterial shrink in a conventional garden realizes that is it extremely hard to destroy the issue. A considerable lot of these pathogens cover up in the dirt until the environments are correct, and afterward they get a move on. In hydroponics, the cultivator can totally wipe out the hydroponic system if there is an instance of a soilborne pathogen. This permits the garden worker to rapidly expel the old yield, clean and disinfect the system, and afterward fire up another harvest.

16. Reduces capability of tainting crops

A few of the national foodborne infection episodes have been followed back to fertilizer. Animal compost, one of the essential supplement contributions on customary ranches, is a potential wellspring of destructive pathogens, including E. coli, Listeria, also, Salmonella, if not appropriately arranged before application. The issue is that not all fertilizers present in agrarian fields are applied by the rancher. In 2011, an E. coli episode in Oregon was accepted to be because of deer defecation found on the speculated ranch. It is uncommon to perceive any excrement inferred manures in hydroponics, and tainting from untamed life is exceptionally phenomenal, as most hydroponic homesteads are in controlled situations that prohibit natural life.

Disadvantages and Challenges

1. A Hydroponic garden requires your time and duty

Much the same as any things advantageous throughout everyday life, dedicated and mindful demeanor gives acceptable yields. In any case, in soil-borne partners, plants can be left all alone for quite a long time and weeks, they despite everything make due in a brief timeframe. The unstoppable force of life and soils will help manage if something isn't adjusting. That is not the situation in Hydroponics. Plants will cease to exist all the more rapidly without appropriate consideration and satisfactory information. Recollect that your plants are relying upon you for their endurance. You should take great consideration of your plants, and the system upon beginning establishment. At that point you can computerize the entire thing later, yet you despite everything need to measure and forestall the sudden issues of the activities, and do visit upkeep.

2. Encounters and specialized information

You are running an arrangement of numerous kinds of hardware, which requires important explicit skill for the gadgets utilized, what plants you can develop and how they can endure and flourish in a soilless situation. Mistakes in setting up the system s and plants' development capacity right now and you wind up demolishing your entire advancement.

3. Natural discussions

There have been some warmed contentions about whether Hydroponics ought to be ensured as natural or not. Individuals are addressing whether plants developed hydroponically will get microbiomes as they are in the dirt. Be that as it may, individuals around the globe have developed hydroponic plants - lettuces, tomatoes, strawberries, and so forth for many years, particularly in Australia, Tokyo, Netherland, and the United States. They have given nourishment to a huge number of individuals. You can't anticipate flawlessness from anything throughout everyday life. In any event, for soil developing, there are still more dangers of pesticides, bothers, and so forth contrasted with Hydroponics. There are some natural developing techniques recommended for Hydroponic cultivators. For instance, a few producers give microbiomes to plants by utilizing natural developing media, for example, coco coir and include worm throwing into it. Regular made Nutrients are generally utilized, for example, angles, bones, hay, cottonseeds, neems, and so on.

For this discussion for the natural item issue, there will at present be inquires about done right now and sooner rather than later. Furthermore, we'll know the appropriate response at that point.

4. Water and power dangers

In a Hydroponic system, for the most part you use water and power. Be careful with power in a blend of water in nearness. Continuously put wellbeing first when working with the water system s and electric hardware, particularly in business gardens.

5. System disappointment dangers

You are utilizing power to deal with the entire system. So assume you don't take fundamental activities for a force blackout, the system will quit working promptly, and plants may dry out rapidly and will kick the bucket in a few hours. Subsequently, a reinforcement power source and plan ought to consistently be arranged, particularly for extraordinary scale system s.

6. Introductory costs

You make certain to spend under one hundred to a couple many dollars (contingent upon your garden scale) to buy gear for your first establishment. Whatever system s you fabricate, you will require compartments, lights, a pump, a clock, developing media, Nutrients). When the system has been set up, the cost will be diminished to just Nutrients and power (to keep the water system running, and lighting).

7. Long return per speculation

If you follow news on farming beginning up, you may have realized that there have been some new indoor hydroponic business began as of late. That is something beneficial for the horticulture division and the improvement of Hydroponics also. Be that as it may, business producers despite everything face some enormous difficulties when beginning with Hydroponics for a huge scope. This is to a great extent a result of the high starting costs and the long, unsure ROI (rate of profitability). It is difficult to detail an unmistakable gainful arrangement to encourage for venture while there are likewise numerous other alluring cutting edge fields out there that appear to be genuinely encouraging for financing.

8. Illnesses and vermin may spread rapidly

You are developing plants in a shut system utilizing water. On account of plant diseases or vermin, they can raise quick to plants on a similar supplement repository. As a rule, maladies and irritations are less of issue in a little arrangement of home producers.

So couldn't care less much about these issues if you are fledglings.

It's confounded for enormous hydroponic gardens. So better to have a decent malady the executives plan heretofore. For instance, utilize simply clean sickness free water sources and developing materials; checking the system s intermittently, and so forth.

Should the ailments occur, you have to sanitize the tainted water, supplement, and the entire system quick.

Chapter Three: Lighting And Heat Types Of Hydroponics System

LIGHT QUALITY AND INTENSITY

Light capture attempt by the plant shelter is affected by the leaf zone presented to incoming radiation with plant dividing significantly affecting block attempt. One of the essential reasons why garden tomato yields far surpass that reachable for field-developed plants is the more noteworthy block attempt of light energy because of the expanded leaf territory records of the garden plants. The estimation of the lower leaves on the tomato plant is impressive as far as their commitment to plant development and organic product yield.

High light force is likely as impeding to tomato natural product creation as low light power may be. With high sun powered radiation affecting natural product, breaking, sunscald, and green shoulders can be the outcome. What's more, high light power can raise the shelter temperature, bringing about poor plant execution. In southern scopes and throughout the mid-year months in all scopes, garden concealing is basic to keep up creation of top notch natural product. Under low light environments, light supplementation is increasingly powerful by expanding the long stretches of light instead of endeavoring to build light force during the daylight hours.

Plants react to both light force and quality. When there is overabundance blue light with next to no red light, the development will be abbreviated, hard, and dull in shading; if there is abundance red light over blue light, the development will turn out to be delicate with internodes long, bringing about thin plants. The tomato plants in the glass-secured house were tall and light green in shading, while those in the fiberglass-secured house were short and dim green in shading; the distinctions in plant appearance were expected to a limited extent to wavelength light sifting. Be that as it may, organic product yields and quality were similar in the two houses; in spite of the fact that in the fiberglass-secured house, the social necessities were simpler to deal with shorter plants.

Utilization of counterfeit light to develop plants can be followed back to the 1800s. Develop lights were not constantly a commonsense alternative, yet in the previous scarcely any decades there have been propels in lighting innovation that have utilized develop lights available to diversion garden workers with gardens of any size. There are many lighting choices, however not all are appropriate for your particular developing zone; if you don't mind survey the numerous alternatives before buying a develop light to maintain a strategic distance from a possibly exorbitant Mistake.

Fluorescent: These are likely the most novice cordial develop lights.

They are additionally generally accessible and moderately modest contrasted with other develop lights.

They devour negligible power and are accessible in a few ranges, so you can grow a wide scope of yields. They may not be perfect for crops that require serious light, for example, peppers. Since they discharge just modest quantities of heater, they can be put near the yield—inside several inches—which makes them incredible for seedlings and youthful plants.

High Pressure Sodium (HPS): These are perhaps the least expensive choice for high-power lighting. HPS lights can produce a great deal of heater, which is acceptable in chilly situations yet hard to oversee inside without appropriate ventilation as well as cooling. They frequently are utilized for flowering crops inside and are incredible for giving supplemental light in gardens. Normally they are situated a couple of feet over a yield.

Metal Halide (MH) and Ceramic Metal Halide (CMH): MH and CMH are high-force lighting alternatives regularly utilized for vegetative stages but at the same time are fit for developing Flowering crops. Light from MH bulbs seems blue and numerous garden workers think that its lovely to work under. The blue predominant light is additionally useful for empowering minimized development. Most develop light makers are concentrating creation on the more current, increasingly effective CMH bulbs rather than the customary MH bulbs.

Light Emitting Diodes (LEDs): LEDs are exceptionally effective, utilizing insignificant power to produce a ton of light. They produce next to no heater comparative with their light yield and are accessible in a wide range of arrangements, some appropriate for mounting high over the harvest and some reasonable for setting extremely near the harvest. LEDs come in a wide range of hues, which can significantly influence plant development. The white LEDs are less productive however more charming to work under than red and blue LEDS, which cast a purple light that is incredible for developing plants yet a few cultivators find tastefully disappointing.

Extra Light Options Other choices incorporate enlistment lights, plasma lights, and lasers, just as numerous other lighting advancements other than the ones recorded previously. A portion of these more up to date lighting choices can be over the top expensive and may not be appropriate for the starting hydroponic plant specialist. Lighting innovation propels rapidly, be that as it may, and huge numbers of these alternatives may before long be the standard, similarly as LED lighting is rapidly moving to the front line among the conventional HPS, MH, and fluorescent lighting choices.

Lighting Accessories

Holders Lights: can be hung with rope, link, or bind or mounted legitimately to a crossbeam or the roof. Rope ratchets are exceptionally well known with indoor garden workers since they make moving lights all over extremely simple.

Develop Room Glasses: Some plant specialists think that it's disagreeable to work under the orange light of HPS or the purple light of LED develop lights. Glasses with tinted Unit points planned explicitly for these light sources are an extraordinary method to make it progressively wonderful to work with these develop lights.

Heating arrangements

Greenhouse heating is required in chilly climate environments, wherein the ensnared heat isn't adequate for plant development during the evenings. The Heating system must give heater to the Greenhouse at a similar rate at which it is lost by conduction, penetration, and radiation. There are three mainstream sorts of heating system s for gardens.

• Unit heater s.

• Central heater s.

• Radiant heater s.

There is a fourth conceivable sort of system, however it has picked up practically no spot in the Greenhouse business: sunlight based Heating system. Sun oriented Heating is still too costly to possibly be a suitable choice. A few options in contrast to traditional Heating techniques are heat pumps, biomass system s, and co-age system s. A correlation of these to ordinary system s shows that bio-mass and co-age system s offer significant advantages all through the state, while the possibility of heater pumps relies upon power rates and, subsequently, on the geographic area of the Greenhouse. Just the heater pump change local will be treated in the present. Heater or warm air is circulated from the unit heater s by one of two normal techniques: the convection-tube strategy or HAF, like winter cooling system s (Nelson, 1998).

Unit heater system

The most widely recognized and most affordable is the unit heater system. Right now, air is blown from unit heater s that have independent fireboxes. Heater s are situated all through the Greenhouse, each Heating a story zone 2000 to 6000 ft2 (186 to 558 m2). These heater s comprise of three practical parts, to be specific, firebox, metal cylinder heat exchanger, and heater conveyance fan. Fuel is combusted in a firebox to give heat. The heater is at first contained in the fumes, which ascends through within a lot of flimsy walled metal cylinders on its way to the fumes stack. The warm fumes moves heater to the cooler metal dividers of the cylinders. A significant part of the heater is expelled from the fumes when it arrives at the stack through which it leaves the Greenhouse. A fan in the rear of the unit warmer attracts Greenhouse air, disregarding it the outside side of the cylinders and afterward out the front of the heater to the Greenhouse environment once more. The cool air ignoring hot metal cylinders is warmed and the air is coursed (Radha and Igathinathane, 2007).

Unit radiators are the most normally utilized type of Heating because of the accompanying reasons (NGMA, 1998):

• They give the air course required.

• They can be joined with ventilation systems and waste heater applications.

• They can give uniform seat top/under temperatures.

• They are equivalently the most affordable.

• They give snappy reaction to temperature changes.

• They are anything but difficult to introduce.

• They offer economical extension for increments.

• They give snow load assurance which encourages sun powered addition and plant development.

Central heat framework

A second kind of framework is Central Heating framework, which comprises of a Central kettle that produces steam or boiling water, in addition to an emanating component in the garden to disseminate the heat. A Central Heating framework can be more effective than unit warmers, particularly in enormous garden ranges. Right now, or all the more enormous boilers are in a solitary area. Heat is shipped as boiling water or steam through channel mains to the developing territory, and a few game plans of heating pipes in garden.

The heat is traded from the boiling water in a funnel curl on the border dividers in addition to an overhead channel loop situated over the garden or an in-bed pipe curl situated in the plant zone. A few gardens have a third funnel loop installed in a solid floor. A lot of unit radiators can be utilized in the spot of the overhead channel loop, getting heat from high temp water or steam from the Central evaporator.

Radiant heat framework

Right now, is scorched inside channels suspended overhead in the garden. The warm channels transmit heat to the plants. Low force infrared Radiant warmers can spare 30% or a greater amount of fuel contrasted with customary radiators. A few of these radiators are introduced couple in the garden. Lower air temperatures are conceivable since just the plants and root substrate are warmed legitimately by this method of Heating (Radha and Igathinathane, 2007).

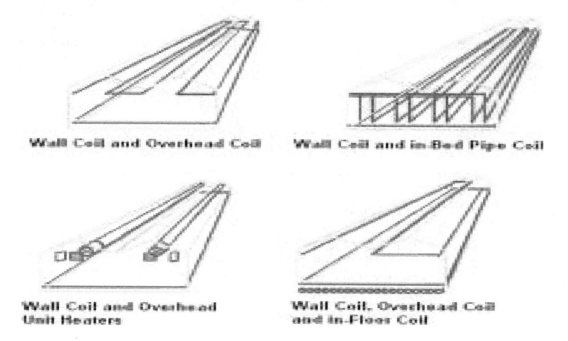

Wall Coil and Overhead Coil   Wall Coil and in-Bed Pipe Coil

Wall Coil and Overhead   Wall Coil, Overhead Coil
Unit Heaters   and in-Floor Coil

Change from fuel to warm energy happens similarly as in an evaporator or unit warmer. A little burner warms the air in an ignition chamber. The sight-seeing is then dispersed in a round steel tube which for the most part runs down the length of the garden, close to the pinnacle. The heat energy is then moved legitimately to the plants and the developing surface through electro-attractive waves going at the speed of light. The plants and developing surfaces at that point retain this energy and convert it into heat, therefore warming the plants and soil. Infrared frameworks are anything but difficult to introduce in numerous applications and can furnish a situation with warm dry leaves (NGMA, 1998).

Solar Heating framework

Solar Heating frameworks are found in side interest gardens and little business firms. Both water and Gravel energy stockpiling frameworks are utilized in blend with sun powered energy. The significant expense of sun oriented Heating frameworks disheartens any critical use by the garden businesses.

Sun oriented Heating is frequently utilized as a halfway or all out option in contrast to petroleum derivative heating frameworks. Hardly any sunlight based Heating frameworks exist in gardens today. The general parts of sunlight based Heating framework, appeared in Figure 5.101 are gatherer, heat storeroom, exchanger to move the sun powered determined Heat to the garden air, reinforcement warmer to assume control over when sun oriented Heating doesn't do the trick, and set of controls.

Different sun oriented Heat authorities are in presence, yet the sort that has gotten most noteworthy consideration is the level plate gatherer. This comprises of a level dark plate (unbending plastic, film plastic, sheet metal, or board) for retaining sun powered energy. The plate is secured on the sun side by at least two straightforward glass or plastic layers and on the posterior by protection. The encasing layers serve to hold the gathered Heat inside the gatherer. Water or air is disregarded through or the dark plate to ingest the ensnared Heat and convey it to the storeroom. A garden itself can be considered as a sun powered authority. A portion of its gathered Heat is put away in the dirt, plants, garden casing, floor, etc. The staying inordinate Heat not required for plant development is subsequently vented to the outside. The abundance vented Heat could similarly too be coordinated to a stone bed for capacity and resulting use during a time of Heating. Assortment of Heat by level plate authorities is most effective when the gatherer is situated opposite to the sun beams at sun powered early afternoon. In view of the areas, the Heat inferred can give 20 to half of the Heat prerequisite (Radha and Igathinathane, 2007).

Heat pump

Heat pumps use power to move heat from the outside environment to within the garden. A natural liquid or refrigerant, for example, dichlorodifluoromethane (R-12) or 1,1,1,2-

tetrafluoroethane (R-134a) is gone through a heat exchanger, where it assimilates energy from the outside environment and disintegrates. This fume is packed and afterward went during a time heat exchanger (condenser) inside the garden. The fume gathers and discharges heat. The high-pressure fluid comes back to a supply and afterward through an extension valve back to the evaporator.

Power drives the blower, fans, and pumps in the heat pump framework. The warm energy source can be the outside air, groundwater, surface water, the dirt, or direct Radiant energy. Heat from the pump can be created as warmed air or high temp water. Since most heat pumps use power, their boundless reception could actuate a heap move for electric utilities, expanding power request around evening time and in the winter, and diminishing petroleum gas utilization.

Chapter Four: How To Setup Your Own System At Home

The most effective method to Build a Homemade Hydroponics System

Hydroponic gardens are anything but difficult to begin in your own home so you can develop consistently. There are a wide range of styles of gardens you can fabricate, the most well-known being wick frameworks, profound water societies, and supplement film procedures. With a basic form, you can undoubtedly have a garden in your home!

Making a Simple Wick System

1 . Cut the best 4 in (10 cm) off of a plastic jug. Reuse a void 1⁄2 US lady (1.9 L) soft drink bottle. Start your cut with a couple of scissors or utility blade simply over the container's name, or around 4 inches (10 cm) down from the top. Cut around the whole jug until the top is totally removed.

- Utilizing a soft drink jug will hold 1 plant. If you need to house 10 or less plants in a hydroponic garden, think about utilizing a 20 US lady (76 L) plastic tote.

2 . Jab an opening through the jug top utilizing a screwdriver. Set the jug top on a hard surface, for example, a cutting board. Hold the top by its sides with your non-prevailing hand while you perforate the inside with a screwdriver. Make the gap about 1⁄4 in (0.64 cm) wide.

- Heat the finish of the screwdriver over a light fire to dissolve the plastic top If you experience difficulty punching through it.
- In case you're utilizing a plastic tote, utilize a gap saw connection for a drill to make 3-4 openings along the center of the top.

3. Feed a bit of twine through the opening in the top. Cut a bit of twine with a couple of scissors so it's around 12 in (30 cm) long. Feed the finish of the twine through the highest point of the container top until you have around 6 in (15 cm) on each side. When the twine is through the top, screw it back onto the bottle.

- In case you're utilizing a bigger store, you may utilize a thicker bit of rope as the wick to ship more water.

4. Fill the base of the container with a supplement arrangement. Visit your neighborhood planting store to locate a supplement blend implied for hydroponic cultivating. You can utilize a similar arrangement paying little mind to what you plant in your framework. Fill the base of your jug with around 4 c (950 ml) of faucet water. Follow the headings on your supplement answer for discover the sum you have to mix into your water. When you include the perfect sum, blend the water in with a mix stick.

Use locally acquired cleaned water in your holder if you have hard faucet water.

If you can't locate any supplement blends coming up, request a jug on the web.

5. Spot the highest point of the jug topsy turvy so the twine is for the most part submerged. When you have the supplement arrangement combined, set the highest point of the jug topsy turvy so the top faces down. Ensure there's around 1 inch (2.5 cm) of twine between the container top and the highest point of the solution.

- In case you're utilizing a plastic tote, utilize a plastic compartment that is 3–4 in (7.6– 10.2 cm) profound over the tote cover. Make a point to bore gaps in the new plastic holder so they line up with the openings in your tote.

6. Put developing medium and your seeds into the highest point of the container. Search for a medium that permits water and Nutrients to effectively go through it, for example, perlite, coconut coir, or vermiculite. Spread 2 bunches of the medium in the top bit of the container and pack it daintily with your fingers. After the developing medium is included, you can plant your seeds at the profundity indicated on their packaging.

Each developing medium can be bought from your neighborhood cultivating or yardcare store. Any of these developing mediums will work regardless of which plants you're utilizing.

The supplement arrangement goes up the wick into the developing medium to give nourishment and water to your plants.

Wick frameworks work extraordinary for new hydroponic cultivators and are hands-off, however they can't bolster bigger plants. Wick frameworks work best for herbs or lettuce.

Tip: Plant at any rate 3 seeds to expand your odds of fruitful germination. When 1 of the plants develops in more than the others, meager out the more fragile developments.

2. Building a Deep Water Culture System

1. Cut an opening in the top of a plastic espresso holder a similar size as a net pot. Net pots have spaces so water can without much of a stretch move through them. Follow the base of your net pot onto the espresso compartment top with a pencil or marker. Utilize a specialty blade or an utility blade to slice the gap to estimate so the pot fits firmly inside the pattern segment. Keep on shaving the sides away until the edge of the net pot is level with the highest point of the lid.

- A coffee container can hold 1 plant. If you need to make a bigger hydroponic garden, utilize a huge plastic tote rather with different net pots.

2. Cut a little X close to the edge of the top for an air tube. Measure in about 1/2 in (1.3 cm) from the edge of the cover and imprint the spot with a pen or marker. Push your art blade through the cover to make a cut. Turn the cover by 90 degrees and make another cut experiencing the principal one.

- Make your cut like the opening where you put a straw in on a cheap food drink cover.

3. Feed 6 in (15 cm) of air tubing through the X. Utilize 1/4–1/2 in (0.64–1.27 cm) tubing in your profound water culture framework. Stick the finish of the cylinder through the X-shape you cut until you've taken care of in 6 in (15 cm) or until the cylinder arrives at the base of the holder. Leave enough tubing on top to arrive at a bubbler machine, or around 1 1/2 feet (46 cm).

4. Fill the espresso compartment seventy five percent full with a supplement arrangement. Supplement blends are sold at cultivating stores or on the web, and any blend will work paying little mind to what you're planting. Fill the espresso compartment seventy five percent full with faucet water. Follow the headings on the mark cautiously to blend the perfect measure of the supplement fluid for the measure of water you use. Utilize a mixing stick to consolidate the Nutrients with the water. Set the top back on your espresso container.

- If you have hard faucet water, use locally acquired cleaned water in your compartment.

5. Put developing medium and seeds into the net pot. Fill the pot to the top with either coconut coir, perlite, or vermiculite. Sow the seeds of your plant about 1/2 in (1.3 cm) somewhere down in your developing medium.

- Pick verdant greens or herbs when planting seeds rather than bigger plants.
- Any of the developing mediums will work paying little mind to the sort of plant you're developing.
- Seed profundity while planting may change contingent upon the kind of plant. Counsel with the seed bundle to check whether they should be planted shallower or more profound.

6. Append the opposite finish of the air cylinder to a bubbler and turn it on. Bubblers help add oxygen to the arrangement so your foundations don't suffocate. Secure the finish of your tubing standing out from the highest point of the holder to the port on the bubbler, and turn it on. Leave the bubbler on the whole time while your plants are growing.

- The supplement arrangement douses into the developing medium in your pot, furnishing your plants with consistent water and nourishment so they can develop.
- Profound water supplement frameworks are low-upkeep and simple to make at home, however they don't function admirably for plants that have a long developing period.
- Bubblers can be bought from your nearby pet or aquarium store.
- Bubblers need to run consistently or else your plants could bite the dust.

3. Utilizing the Nutrient Film Technique

1. Associate a pump to an air stone on the base of the water repository. Make a gap 2 in (5.1 cm) down from the highest point of a 20 US lady (76 L) plastic tote with an utility blade. Set an air stone in your tote on a similar side with the gap and feed the air tube through it. Append the tubing to an air pump.

- Pneumatic machines and air stones can be bought from your neighborhood pet or aquarium store.

2. Set a submersible water pump on the opposite side of the store. Set the water pump on the contrary side of the tote as the air stone. Cut an opening on the tote that is 2–3 in (5.1–7.6 cm) down from the top and enormous enough for the force link and 1/2 in (1.3 cm) tubing. Feed the cylinder and the force line through the hole.

- Water pumps can be bought from your nearby pet store.

3. Fill a large portion of the store with a supplement arrangement. Use around 10 gallons (38 L) of tap or sanitized water in your tote so your pump and air stone are totally submerged. Any supplement blend can be utilized paying little heed to the plants you're developing. Include the measure of supplement fluid recorded on the name for the water in your tote. Combine the arrangement with a mix stick.

Supplement fluids can be purchased from your neighborhood garden store or on the web.

4. Slant a downpour canal or PVC pipe between 2 sawhorses to make a channel. Utilize a 4–6 ft (1.2–1.8 m) bit of downpour drain or PVC funneling. Append a 2 in × 4 in (5.1 cm × 10.2 cm) board over one of the sawhorses with 2 screws or nails. Space your sawhorses 3 ft (0.91 m) separated so your tote fits among them, and set the channeling or downpour canal on top.

- Ensure the parts of the bargains are shut so water doesn't spill out.

5. Cut openings in the highest point of your channel to accommodate your pots. Utilize a 2–3 in (5.1–7.6 cm) opening saw connection for your drill to make gaps on the highest point of your channel. Space every one of your plants around 1 ft (30 cm) separated so they have space for the roots to develop. Spot 1 net pot in each gap once they're cut.

- Your channel should fit around 4-6 plants relying upon to what extent it is.
- Gap saw connections can be bought at your nearby home improvement shop. Make a point to pick an opening saw made for the material you're slicing through.
- The size of your gap relies upon the size of the net pots you plan on utilizing.

6. Make a channel opening in the lower end of your channel and the top of your repository. Drill a 1 in (2.5 cm) gap in the base of the channel around 1–1 1/2 in (2.5–3.8 cm) from the edge. Make another 1–2 in (2.5–5.1 cm) gap in the cover of the tote legitimately underneath the channel so the water keeps recycling.

- You can run a cylinder between the channel and the top if you need, yet it's not required.

7. Feed the water pump tube into the higher finish of your channel. Utilize a drill or a gap saw to make a 1/2 in (1.3 cm) opening in the focal point of the raised finish of your channel. Feed the finish of the cylinder 2–3 in (5.1–7.6 cm) into the direct so it remains in securely.

- You may likewise make a gap in the highest point of your channel if you would prefer not to take care of in from the side.
- The size of the opening may rely upon how thick your tubing is.

8. Fill your pots with developing medium and seeds. Utilize a hydroponics-accommodating developing medium, for example, perlite, coconut coir, or vermiculite. Fill each pot so they're seventy five percent full before planting the seeds. Put each seed about 1/4–1/2 in (0.64–1.27 cm) profound into the pot.

Hydroponic cultivating works best for verdant greens or for crisp herbs.

9. Plug in the water pump so it continually runs. Ensure the water pump moves the supplement arrangement through the base of the channel without spilling. The arrangement will course through the channel and the underlying foundations of your plants to furnish them with consistent Nutrients before falling go into your reservoir.

- The supplement film method continually pumps a slight layer of water through the channel so your plants develop without suffocating the roots.

- Supplement film frameworks take into consideration numerous plants to develop and recycle water to diminish squander, yet the pumps need to continually run or else your plants may pass on.
- Attachment the pump into a programmed clock that runs each 2-3 hours If you don't need the pump continually running.

Tip: Plant roots can become long enough to stop up the channel or depletes. Check your channel in any event once per week to ensure everything is as yet streaming appropriately.

Chapter Five: Nutrient Solution And Growing Media

Hydroponic Nutrient Solution-The Essential Guide

Much the same as a parent continually stressing over how to develop their kids best until adulthood, the plants needs your minding to bring the best yields. What's more, Nutrients are the response for both.

Supplement answer for Hydroponic is much the same as fertilizers to soil. Basically, a Hydroponic supplement arrangement is a fluid loaded up with the entirety of the fundamental Nutrients so plant roots can come into contact for its development.

Contrasted with soil, Hydroponic makes it simpler to gauge and fill the specific measures of Nutrients in the water arrangements.

Is there any set equation for these supplement recipes? No is the appropriate response since each plant requires various Nutrients. Additionally, this depends on a great deal of different elements like development stages, climates, etc. Also, various equations have been produced for hydroponics. More often than not, significant Nutrients for plants are the equivalent. Simply the level of them is unique.

What Do Plants Need to Grow?

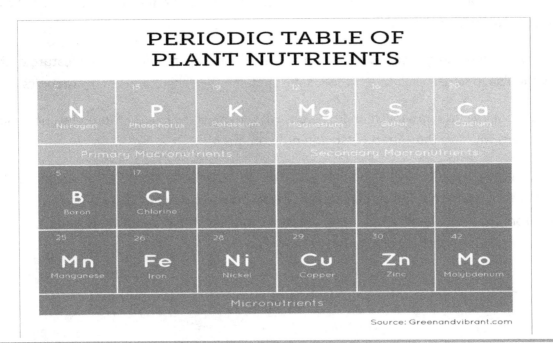

Essential Nutrients

For endurance, plants need to breathe, get dampness and photosynthesize. Also, they are as Oxygen, Carbon, Hydrogen, and Nitrogen. O, C, H, and N are on the whole promptly accessible noticeable all around, water. What's more, plants can get these components from nature. In the interim, lights supply plants with energy to make nourishment.

Also, before furnishing plants with vital Nutrients, you should deal with these natural fertilizers first. Without them, plants will undoubtedly bite the dust. In the interim, without Nutrients, plants can at present live however won't grow appropriately.

Macro Nutrients

These are Nutrients that plants need to ingest in enormous amounts. They are the most indispensable supplement minerals you should deal with first.

Nitrogen

Without questions, Nitrogen is viewed as the most significant components among all the Nutrients. It is fundamentally liable for

- The vegetative development of plants - leaves, stems and their hues.
- Development of Chlorophyll, amino acids, co-chemicals, and proteins utilized in new cell dividers.

Individuals typically utilize a lot of Nitrogen for the development times of plants before they begin bearing Fruits or Flowering.

Since plants need nitrogen so rapidly at certain periods, nitrogen is utilized as a feature of the strengthening materials - manures in soil, and supplement arrangements in hydroponics.

Plants that need nitrogen show manifestations with their yellow leaves. More seasoned and lower leaves will have the impacts first, and drop off quick.

At the point when plants have an abundance of nitrogen, the side effects are more earnestly to perceive. Your plants may look green and energetic, however their capacity to endure foods grown from the ground are incredibly diminished. That is on the grounds that plants are burning through the entirety of its effort creating foliage.

Phosphorus

As a crucial supplement for plants like Nitrogen, Phosphorus is the basic segment of DNA, the hereditary memory unit of plants. That is significant tin issue arrangement and cell division. Phosphorus assumes a basic job in the improvement of

- Flowering
- Fruits
- Seeds
- Roots

Your plants will require a lot of phosphorus at the early period of seedling, germination and blooming stage, but on the other hand it's vital during the entire plants' life cycle.

Plants insufficient of phosphorus show sign of shorter plant development - strange frail leaves, blossoms, and roots.

In the interim, the over the top of phosphorus influence the plants by keeping it from engrossing different components like calcium, copper, iron, magnesium and zinc. So the inadequacies of these components can be seen.

Potassium (K)

Another irreplaceable plant supplement that is required in an enormous sufficient sum for the viable advancement and proliferation of plants.

Potassium doesn't frame mixes in plants like different Nutrients, however it helps mix an assortment of critical procedures including photosynthesis, starch development, protein union, and chemical initiation.

Plants that are needing potassium for the most part show yellow leaves first. When in high of potassium, similar to phosphorus, plants will be not able to interface with different Nutrients, for example, zinc, iron, magnesium.

Calcium

Important to cell arrangement and improvement. Excessively little of calcium, leaf tips, and edges will turn dark colored and can bite the dust. An excessive amount of calcium at the more youthful stage can stunt plant development.

Sulfur

An auxiliary part of two of the 21 amino corrosive that makes protein. Additionally, enacts and structure certain proteins and nutrients.

Magnesium

One of the synthetic segments of chlorophyll. Magnesium makes the oxygen through photosynthesis and is frequently utilized in enormous sums in quickly developing plants.

Among these, The three macronutrients (N, P, K) depicted above are the most urgent Nutrients for plant's improvement.

Micro Nutrients

Micro Nutrients are as yet significant in plant improvement, however they are required in littler amounts.

Zinc

Zinc is significant in the development of chlorophyll and different motors, and nitrogen digestion.

Boron

Boron is utilized with calcium in blending the structure and elements of cell layers. Likewise, help with fertilization and seed creation.

Iron

A part of numerous proteins related with energy arrangement, nitrogen obsession. Help structure chlorophyll, and is utilized in photosynthesis.

Manganese (Mn)

Catalyze the development procedure, and help structure oxygen in photosynthesis.

Choosing and Preparing Nutrient Solutions

You can make your own supplement blend, or get a Hydroponic supplement bundle from the store. For amateurs, I enthusiastically prescribe you to get it, sparing the testing and blending your own Nutrients when you get a piece encounters.

Regularly, you will see recorded in the fixings and recipe of the arrangements sold at the store are 3 numbers in rates. These are the 3 most significant minerals that recorded above - Nitrogen (N), Phosphorus (P), Potassium (K). For instance, they come at the proportion 10-10-

10, implying that each the supplement is made out of 10% of the arrangement. The remainder of 70% is water, Micro Nutrients, and different chelates that help the healthful procedure.

Obviously, that proportion will be extraordinary, contingent upon an assortment of criteria:

- Plants types
- Plant development arrange
- Portions of plants you need to bring the most yields (leaf, natural product, root)
- Light power, climate, temperature, the period of the year.

Here are the recommended nutrient solutions for some plant types

Crop	N	P	K	Ca	Mg
Concentration in mg/l (ppm)					
Tomato	190	40	310	150	45
Cucumber	200	40	280	140	40
Pepper	190	45	285	130	40
Strawberry	50	25	150	65	20
Melon	200	45	285	115	30
Roses	170	45	285	120	40

If you are to pick accessible answers for your hydroponic garden, the one thing to remember is that you ought to get the supplement structured explicitly for Hydroponics as it were. Disregard the universally handy bundle which can be utilized in both soil and hydroponics. Normal fertilizers utilized in soil don't contain fundamental micronutrients that Hydroponics plants require.

Second, it is prescribed to utilize the 2 or 3 sections arrangement in the fluid. Regularly, a fluid arrangement is simpler to work with than powder structure since it effectively processes in water, and a large portion of the fluid arrangement accompanies pH cushions.

Furthermore, you should purchase the 3 section since it helps you later when you have to mix and blend in various mixes for the plant's development reason, and explicit phase of development.

To spare your time, I have handpicked the best hydroponic Nutrients available here

The following are basic strides to blend the 3 sections arrangements, to be specific the 3 section arrangement by General Hydroponics.

1. Check which phases of development your plants are so as to blend the 3 sections in with the right proportion. Check the maker guidance of your supplement items.

2. Start by adding crisp water to the supply.

3. Add the Micro part first to the water. It contains components like Calcium, Copper, Boron, Iron, Manganese and Zinc and some Nitrogen. Mix the arrangement.

4. Next is the Grow part. This contains ammoniacal nitrogen, nitrate nitrogen, phosphate, potassium, and magnesium. Mix well.

5. Include the Bloom Hydroponics arrangement. This contains phosphate, potassium, dissolvable magnesium and sulfur. Once more, mix the arrangement.

6. It's essential to Check the pH of the supplement blend in the wake of getting all Nutrients into your supplement tank. Plants neglect to take up significant Nutrients when the pH level leaves its suggested extend. The perfect one is between 5.5 to 6.5

7. Remember to check the temperature of the arrangement. Around 64 to 66 degrees Fahrenheit is perfect.

Growing Media

Developing media are materials that plants develop in. You for the most part use soil as the developing medium in conventional development. In any case, in Hydroponics, you are not restricted to simply soil.

That is the reason other than spending your attention on finding the best frameworks of Hydroponics in any case, remember to look for appropriate materials for plants to develop. The developing media for your Hydroponics are similarly as significant as the frameworks picked.

For what reason is it so significant?

The developing media are to help furnish plants' foundations with moister and oxygen they need. It likewise underpins the plant weight and holds it upstanding.

Another job of the media is to permit plant's foundations to have most extreme presentation to the supplement. Individuals will moister the developing media with the supplement arrangements. Furthermore, the wet media will move the supplement to the root framework.

Utilizing these media other than soil gives garden workers less stresses over the risk of soil-borne infections and nuisances. This permits them to develop more beneficial and better plants.

You may have heard some developing media like sand, Gravel, peat greenery, perlite, vermiculite. However, the truth of the matter is there are boundless developing media around us. Indeed, even the air can be utilized as a successful developing mode for the roots. Be that as it may, every ha its advantages and disadvantages. Picking a proper developing media is an extremely basic assignment. An ideal one will incredibly affect plants' development and the quality yield. What's more, the inquiry is

What makes an incredible developing medium?

Taking out every single target factor, a perfect medium is the one that

1. Is natural made, biodegradable and ecologically well disposed.

2. Keeps an even proportion of air to water.

3. Has a medium cation-trade ability to hold Nutrients.

4. Shields plants from pH changes after some time.

5. Is reasonable and simple to discover.

6. Is sufficiently lightweight and simple to haul around.

Obviously, it's difficult to fulfill all the criteria you need, however right now, give you important insights regarding the most well known developing media utilized; The favorable circumstances and drawbacks of every material. What's more, in particular, I will assist you with choosing which developing media will fit best for your circumstances.

Hydroponic Growing Media

Perlite

Have you at any point utilized a pack of business gardening soil? Assuming this is the case, you may have seen little white items that appear as though styrofoam balls in the blend.

These little balls are a kind of mineral item called perlite. Each fixing in those blends beneficially affect plants, and perlite is no exemption.

If you need to turn out to be acceptable at cultivating or hydroponics, perlite can be your closest companion. Prepared planters depend on this mineral, and use it broadly in their green undertakings.

Perlite is an extremely regular developing medium that has been around for a considerable length of time, typically utilized by conventional plant specialists to add air circulation to soil blends.

As a mined material, a type of volcanic glass, perlite is made under extreme and fast Heat. At that point endless modest air pockets pop outs like popcorn. So as you can figure, it is lightweight and permeable.

Perlite is a decent decision for the wick-type hydroponic framework since it makes a phenomenal standing wicking activity. But since of its permeable and simple to-stream nature, I don't prescribe utilizing this vehicle for fast and solid watering frameworks like the ebb and stream. It very well may be washed away quick and no problem at all.

Ready to hold air quite well, having nonpartisan pH, however simple to stream, Perlite is once in a while utilized alone. Individuals frequently blend it in with other developing media like vermicule, coco coir or soil - A typical mix is with vermicule in equivalent amount (50-50)

One proviso to working with Perlite is that since this medium is in little and permeable particles, you ought to secure your inward breath when working with. Get it wet heretofore, at that point wash out to shield the residue from rising around.

Advantages:

- Sensibly modest
- Lightweight
- High air maintenance.
- Reusable

Disadvantages:

- Lightweight, not reasonable for certain framework sorts.
- Residue from the medium - impacts on nature and wellbeing

Can be utilized in trickle frameworks, aeroponic frameworks.

Coconut Coir

At the point when you are developing green stuff, it is additionally critical to "remain green." We all know the significance of utilizing environmentally manageable materials to ensure better and save planet earth and its delicate biological systems.

This is the place coconut coir truly sparkles. In addition to the fact that it is a fantastic developing medium, yet it is likewise entirely practical. What's more, it is perfect for both customary gardens just as hydroponics.

Coconut Coir (otherwise called "Cocotek," "Cocopeat" and "Ultrapeat" is basically a result of the coconut business. Individuals make it from the darker husks encompassing the coconut shell. Ultrapeat" is basically a result of the coconut business. Individuals make it from the darker husks encompassing the coconut shell.

What makes this one of the most productive developing media for hydroponics is on the grounds that it is absolutely natural, exceptionally inactive, and holds water well indeed. Yet, it has a great air to water proportion, sparing plants from suffocating.

Coconut coir is well disposed to the earth and sustainable. The unused material can go to removal spots of or be treated the soil.

These cause coconut to turn into a so normally utilized material for Hydroponics as of late.

Coconut Coir can be utilized alone or blended in with other developing media like perlite, extended mud pellets. A typical equation utilized by producers is half of the coconut fiber and half earth pellets.

Advantages:

- Incredible water maintenance and air circulation
- Natural material
- Earth cordial

Disadvantages:

- Uncompressed after a few employments.
- Doesn't deplete well, so regularly blended in with other media.

Can be utilized in trickle frameworks, aquaponic frameworks, back and forth movement framework.

Vermiculite

Vermiculite is a type of hydrated laminar minerals which look like mica.

Much the same as perlite, vermiculite is prepared by presenting the material to extraordinary Heat to extend them into little perfect, unscented pellets.

Vermiculite is an incredible soilless planting medium. It is non-harmful, clean, sodden safe and has an about unbiased pH. Furthermore, the material is exceptionally lightweight and ready to hold water well indeed, which is very differentiating to perlite. However, it doesn't keep air circulation just as perlite.

This developing media likewise has a sensibly extraordinary cation-trade limit, which helps save the Nutrients for sometime in the future.

There are diverse vermiculite types, so remember that and pick the right material for the hydroponic reason.

Furthermore, due to its capacity to hold a lot of water (around 200%-300% of its weight), there's a danger of choking out your plants. So it is typically used to blend in with other media. The most natural one would be perlite as the two media supplement each other very well - perlite depletes so quick though vermiculite holds dampness.

They are regularly conjuncted in a 50/50 equation, which fends the blend from being washed off in rhythmic movement frameworks.

Can be utilized in the trickle framework, aeroponic framework.

Advantages:

Water and supplement maintenance

Disadvantages:

- Poor seepage limit
- Risk of choking out plants

Gravelwool

Gravelwool is a backbone developing media for business hydroponics producers, basically the individuals who execute trickle water system frameworks. Initially utilized as protection and furthermore known as mineral fleece or stone fleece, Gravelwool was created in Denmark, thinking back to the 1970's for cultivating. It holds dampness well, it holds oxygen well, it never obstructs root development, it is artificially inactive, and it arrives in an assortment of sizes and shapes. These advantages add to its notoriety among cultivators, obliging practically any plant they are developing.

Hydroponic producers would not discover Gravelwool that bizarre as this material has been utilized generally as of late, to a great extent on business ranches. What's more, this material has been demonstrated as very viable, and henceforth its prominence.

This clean, permeable medium is basically comprised of stone as well as limestone Gravels which are warmed until dissolving and afterward are spun into excessively thin and long filaments. From that point onward, individuals pack these filaments into 3D squares, blocks of favored sizes.

Gravelwool claims numerous advantages of a perfect developing material like microorganism resistance, great water and air maintenance. This shields your plants from drying out while giving plant roots persistent accessible measures of oxygen.

Be that as it may, there is single word of alert about the pH level when utilizing Gravelwool. The common pH of the material is generally high, which can adjust the supplement arrangement pH. Forestall this by drenching this media into pH adjusted water before utilizing.

Another downside is that Gravelwool is non-degradable and not supportable. The unused strands of Gravelwool are practically incapable to be discarded.

Likewise, the residue emitting from the medium can cause disturbance. This isn't useful for the lungs and eyes, so it's a decent practice to wash it into the water once when utilizing.

From what I heard of late numerous hydroponic specialists quit utilizing it basically due to their feeling of ecological consideration and duty. Numerous cultivators would prefer not to utilize items that bring contaminations from their assembling procedure, and can't be discarded, which is the situation of Gravelwool.

However, Gravelwool is an exceptionally viable developing medium generally.

Advantages:

Extraordinary water assimilation and air circulation limit

Disadvantages:

Not earth benevolent

The residue isn't useful for the wellbeing.

Upset the pH of the supplement arrangement.

Can be utilized in trickle frameworks, back and forth movement frameworks, profound water societies frameworks, supplement film procedure frameworks—practically any framework with the exception of aquaponics.

Extended Clay Pellets or Leca

Hydroton develop shakes, or extended mud pellets, additionally alluded to as leca mud, earth balls, are one of the most supportive and adaptable developing media to any customary and hydroponic cultivator.

They've picked up fame throughout the most recent ten years for their permeable shape. With these pores all through each ball, the pellets make it simple to help a consistent dispersion of Nutrients, oxygen, and water around the underlying foundations of different plants.

Extended dirt pellets or hydroton (lightweight extended earth total) are little round balls, about the size of marbles. They are made by warming and growing muds to frame a great many little air pocket molded balls.

By and large, this is an incredible and powerful developing mode for hydroponic use.

As a type of Gravels, however dirt pellets are lightweight due to its permeable nature. But then they are still overwhelming enough to give solid help for the plants and are very brilliant in wicking up the Nutrients to plants' foundations.

The round and permeable structure makes earth pellets an unfathomably adjusted water to oxygen medium. This unbiased pH medium is reusable. Individuals can clean, sanitize and reuse it.

Earth pellets are not a decent water holding material as a result of the spaces between every pellet. They will deplete and dry out quick. So make certain to get the material watered enough.

Additionally, the pellets are heavier and more costly than other media.

Advantages:

- Reusable, manageable.
- Successful water waste, and air maintenance.

Disadvantages:

- Poor dampness maintenance limit
- More costly than other developing media

Can be utilized in trickle frameworks, back and forth movement frameworks, aquaponic frameworks.

Oasis Cubes

Oasis solid shapes are produced using botanical froth which is planned like a sheet structure. Every one of the medium's individual cell (which appears to be similar to blocks) contains the perfect measure of Nutrients just as air and water for plants' developing.

Producers use desert garden 3D shapes fundamentally as a beginning situation for seedlings or plants' cuttings, not as a full developing medium.

The medium is pH nonpartisan. Its cells assimilate water and air genuinely well, which is exceptionally vital for seeds or cuttings. Likewise, the roots can without much of a stretch develop and extend inside the medium's open cell structure.

Advantages:

- Economical

- Great water and air holding

Disadvantages:

- Not natural
- Not feasible

Utilized for germination and seedling developing stages.

Starter plugs

Starter plugs are another powerful item to begin plant spread or seed germination.

Hydroponic cultivators who care about the earth can discover this item a decent material for thought. They can pick starter plugs that are treated the soil of natural materials.

To make it helpful for the beginning period of planting, starter plugs are regularly made from materials that keep dampness well, are not effectively waterlogged, and simultaneously permits the roots to extend and pass through the free base.

Advantages:

- Incredible for seedlings, and spread
- Practical (contingent upon the material utilized)

Disadvantages:

- Reasonable for seed beginning, or cloning.

- Moderately costly

Rice Hulls

The ordinary result of rice crops and normally discarded material can make great use for soilless developing.

This medium isn't pH unbiased. Last fertilizers for the most part extend from 5.8 to 7.2

Remember not to utilize new rice frames since they are not disinfected, and there are dangers of microorganisms, rotting bugs, and weed seeds. Better to utilize parboiled rice frames (PRH), which has been stemmed, sans rice, dried and clean.

Rice frames can deplete water well. One burden is that the material is deteriorated after some time, so ought to be supplanted all the time.

Advantage:

- Absolutely natural

Disadvantages:

- Separate after some time
- Not pH unbiased

Pumice

Pumice is a mined mineral simply like perlite and is framed by a super-warmed and exceptionally constrained well of lava.

It tends to be white, pale dark or light yellow, contingent upon the zone's minerals. Be that as it may, as a rule, pumice is darker than perlite.

This is a lightweight stone, which is permeable, slow to separate and holds the air well as a result of spaces between every molecule. This makes the medium will in general buoy on water, however not to the degree of perlite.

Pumice has great water maintenance, however not in the same class as vermiculite, which is likewise a mined mineral.

Advantages:

- Lightweight.
- Phenomenal air holding limit

Disadvantages:

- Lightweight for some hydroponic framework

Growstones

Growstones are produced using reused glass from landfills or glass gathering and preparing places.

A few people may stress that they can get cut from this medium since they are produced using glass. Try not to get stressed over that in light of the fact that these reused glass has been not really squashed, soften, at times blended in some calcium carbonates.

This medium is lightweight, exceptionally permeable or more all, it has incredible air circulation, and normal dampness maintenance to the root framework.

You should begin by washing and flush the medium altogether to expel little particles, and residue.

The medium is perfect for utilizing alone or for blending into peat, coco coir and other developing media.

Advantages:

- Lightweight
- Great air to water proportion
- Manageable

Disadvantages:

- Stick to certain roots, which can cause pull harm for some plant types.
- A tad of residue.
- More costly than other media.

Sawdust

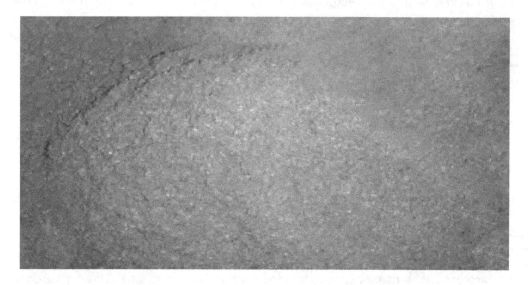

Sawdust is a result of sawmills and retail home improvement shops. It is very cheap, and even you can discover or request free. This material is lightweight, yet holds water well so be certain not to water it. Sawdust is biodegradable yet will deteriorate after some time. This medium isn't pH nonpartisan. So additional consideration of pH checking for your framework needs taking.

Single word of alert is that you should know what sorts of wood your sawdust is made - is it synthetically treated and defiled? This is completely undesirable if you are developing consumable nourishment on this medium. So twofold check about that, and if it has concoction treatment, ensure it is cleaned before use.

Numerous Hydroponic cultivators don't care for sawdust since it compacts rapidly, pH-adjusting, and can be defiled. Be that as it may, sawdust has some restricted achievements in Africa for soilless planting, and for Hydroponic tomato developing in Australia.

Advantages:

- Natural
- economical.

Disadvantages:

- pH whimsical
- Spoil after some time, and can cause microbes.
- May not be sterile

Wood Chips/Fibers

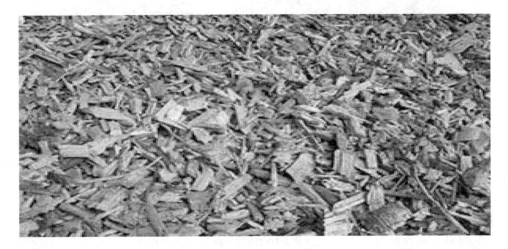

Much the same as sawdust, wood chips or strands are from woods. So they are absolutely natural, an incredible alternative for cultivators who have an eco-accommodating outlook. What's more, again ensure that wood chips are not utilized from defiled wood, or ought to be sanitized before utilizing.

Wood chips hold water well. In any case, it isn't so compacted and waterlogged as sawdust.

Advantage:

- Absolutely natural
- Ready to hold water well.

Disadvantages:

- Biodegradable
- Can contain synthetic compounds.
- May bring parasites, bothers.

Peat Moss

You may have seen that dull darker stringy material called "Peat Moss" in your dad's garden or any garden and garden stores.

In any case, did you realize that however Peat Moss is valuable as a planting medium and is utilized a great deal either as fertilized soil blend or as a hydroponic developing medium, it mixes loads of natural questionable talk?

Bunches of cultivators, even the individuals who use it much regularly, don't know altogether what Peat Moss is, the manner by which it begins, how to appropriately utilize this material in the garden, and comprehend what this medium way to the earth.

Soil Gardening sweethearts would locate this material very recognizable as an amazing dampness supplement holding, and natural soil-relaxing sturdy material. In any case, Peat greenery likewise makes great use in Hydroponics whether alone, or related to other material.

Peat greenery is a dead stringy material that creates in a wet, cool, acidic, and absence of-air condition called peat marshes. In that condition, sphagnum greenery and other living things disintegrate into a thick dull darker conservative. This is the peat greenery. This procedure takes spot such a long time, even two or three a huge number of years. So peat greenery isn't viewed as a sustainable medium, and not well disposed to the earth.

This is a decent vehicle for soil and hydroponic planting due to Its capacity to hold water and hold Nutrients well. Peat greenery can get wet then rehydrate speedy and doesn't conservative or separate no problem at all. These keep the material's life pattern of quite a long while of utilization.

In addition, the medium doesn't contain unfavorable weed seeds or microorganisms, in contrast to other natural manure.

Individuals can mix peat greenery with perlite, vermiculite, or styrofoam particles to include air circulation and change the PH of this medium.

Advantages:

- Great water, and supplement holding.
- Doesn't smaller
- Doesn't involve hurtful microorganisms or weeds

Disadvantages:

- Not inexhaustible.
- Low pH, acidic.
- Generally costly

Sand

Soil and hydroponic producers would not discover sand any new as it is one of the most abundant materials on earth and are in extraordinary use for development, street building, glass industry, and so on just as for developing.

That is the motivation behind why sand is individually modest or accessible for nothing at places like the sea shore.

Sand is made out of very little finely separated Gravels. Their molecule size is extremely minor, so water doesn't dry out quick.

Individuals can utilize sand as an incredible beginning medium and afterward attempt with other media as this media is very substantial, and has poor air circulation characteristics, and should typically be cleaned.

You can blend it in with vermiculite, perlite, or coconut to expand the medium's air circulation.

Advantages:

- Modest (or free).

Disadvantages:

- Substantial
- Low air circulation
- The modest size which can hinder some framework types.

Gravel

This developing medium has been being used very ahead of schedule with incredible achievement. The mainstream one is the Gravel based ebb and stream framework.

As divided media from hard-wearing Gravels like sandstone, limestone, or basalt., spaces between every molecule are very enormous. This helps give an ample inventory of air to the roots. And yet, that implies the medium doesn't hold water well, which can make plants' foundations dry out rapidly.

Since Gravel is Gravels, its weight makes a Gravel based framework, particularly enormous one difficult to convey. In any case, that accompanies a preferred position that is tough and can be reusable.

For any length of time that you clean and wash it, you can begin utilizing for first time developing or reusing.

Much the same as sand, this is a decent modest starter mode for soilless developing, at that point individuals can proceed onward to other developing materials.

Advantage:

- Modest (or free).

Disadvantages:

- Poor water maintenance, not appropriate for overwhelming plant roots.
- Overwhelming

Air

Unusually as it sounds, yet hydroponic plants can live with no developing media. In some hydroponic frameworks like aeroponics, plant establishes are hung uninhibitedly noticeable all around and are occasionally saturated with water and supplement through splashes.

So it implies that plants can develop noticeable all around without any issues as long as you furnish it with enough air, water, and supplement.

Plants developed noticeable all around have a major bit of leeway that their root can gain admittance to a lot of oxygens (which absolutely comes at no expense).

Then again, this makes plants thoroughly depend their life on the framework. Assume there is a force cut, a pump or clock disappointment, you can figure that the roots will dry out rapidly, and the passing of plants can be normal.

Advantage:

- A lot of oxygen.

Disadvantages:

- Plant threat in case of-of intensity, pump, clock disappointment

Can be utilized in supplement film procedure frameworks, profound water culture frameworks.

Chapter Six: Best Plant For Hydroponic Gardening And Nutrition

TOMATOES

Numerous sorts of tomatoes, including customary and cherry ones, have been developed broadly by Hydroponic specialists and business cultivators. Organically, the tomato is a natural product, yet the vast majority whether merchants or buyers think about it as vegetables. One thing to remember is that tomatoes require a lot of light. So be set up to buy some develop lights If you need to develop inside.

Lettuces

Lettuces, the ideal element for the plate of mixed greens sandwich in your kitchen, are likely the most widely recognized vegetables that are developed in Hydroponics. They develop very quick in a hydroponic framework and are genuinely simple to deal with. Lettuces can be developed in any Hydroponics framework, including the NFT, Aeroponics, Ebb and Flow, and so forth. This vegetable is no uncertainty an incredible plant if you simply start with Hydroponics.

Spinaches

Spinach leaves

The most loved vegetable that can be either eaten crude or prepared in your supper grows well in the water-based condition. Spinach is a cool plant, so it doesn't require an excess of light. You can gather it at the same time or remove a few leaves. You can find a workable pace a long time of constant reaping under a decent state of atmosphere and developing condition.

Cucumbers

Cucumbers are a typical vining plant that is developed at home and in the business gardens. They appreciate a fast development under adequate condition and consequently give significant returns. There are a few kinds and sizes of cucumbers, including the tough American slicers, long touchy seedless European, and the smooth-cleaned Lebanese cucumbers. All can develop well in Hydroponics. Cucumber is a warm plant so make certain to supply it with enough light and temperature.

Radishes

Radishes are another vegetable that makes a decent enhancing blend in with different vegetables. Radishes are perhaps the most effortless vegetable to develop - either in soil or hydroponics. It's smarter to begin from seeds, and you can see seedlings inside 3 - 7 days. Radishes flourish in cool temperatures and needn't bother with any lights.

Beans

One of the most profitable and low-support vegetables that can be developed hydroponically. You can pick the sorts of beans you can develop, including green beans, shaft beans, pinto beans, lima beans. You will require a trellis or something to help the plants if you plant post beans. Seed germination generally takes 3 - 8 days. Gathering starts following 6 - two months. From that point forward, you can proceed with the harvest for 3 - 4 months.

Blueberries

Blueberries, an extraordinary organic product high in nutrients for your feast, can be developed well in Hydroponics. This plant takes more time to tolerate organic products than strawberries, frequently until the subsequent years. They are generally developed in a NFT framework. It's difficult to plant blueberries from seeds, so transplants are suggested.

Peppers

Hydroponic sweet peppers

Peppers need the equivalent hydroponic developing condition like tomatoes - warm temperature and a lot of lights. Peppers frequently take a few months to develop

You can either begin developing them from seeds or plants from the neighborhood garden provider. Prescribed assortments for hydroponically developing are Jalapeno, Habanero for hot peppers; Mazurka, Cubico, Nairobi, Fellini for sweet peppers.

Chives

It's simpler to develop chives from a plant in a Hydroponic framework. So better to get them from your nearby garden supplies. Under a standard developing condition, it takes six to about two months before it is completely full grown. At that point you can reap it normally - it needs 3 - after a month to completely regrow. Chive requires loads of light, 12 - 14 hours of light every day.

Basil

Basil flourishes very well in a hydroponic framework, and it is without a doubt among the most developed herbs in Hydroponic. You can develop basil in NFT or Drip framework. When this plant arrives at the develop organize, you reap and trim it week by week. Basil needs loads of lights. It will experience a poor development when you don't give it more than 11 hours of lightning.

Mints

Mints, for the most part peppermint and spearmint, have been developed widely whether in soils and hydroponics. Their fragrant mixes in mints are reviving, and sharp, which demonstrates their utilization as a flavor for nourishment and refreshments. Mint roots spread so rapidly, making it perfect to develop with Hydroponics.

Chapter Seven: Best Fruits/ Best Vegetables

Vegetables

1. Lettuces

Great temp: cool. pH: 6.0 - 7.0

Lettuces, the ideal element for the plate of mixed greens sandwich in your kitchen, are likely the most widely recognized vegetables that are developed in Hydroponics. They develop very quick in a hydroponic framework and are genuinely simple to deal with. Lettuces can be developed in any Hydroponics framework, including the NFT, Aeroponics, Ebb and Flow, and so forth. This vegetable is no uncertainty an incredible plant if you simply start with Hydroponics.

2. TOMATOES

Ideal temp: hot. pH: 5.5 - 6.5

Numerous sorts of tomatoes, including customary and cherry ones, have been developed broadly by Hydroponic specialists and business cultivators. Organically, the tomato is a natural product, yet the vast majority whether merchants or buyers think about it as vegetables. One thing to remember is that tomatoes require a lot of light. So be set up to buy some develop lights If you need to develop inside.

3. Radishes

Good temp: cool. pH: 6.0 - 7.0

Radishes are another vegetable that makes a decent enhancing blend in with different vegetables. Radishes are perhaps the most effortless vegetable to develop - either in soil or hydroponics. It's smarter to begin from seeds, and you can see seedlings inside 3 - 7 days. Radishes flourish in cool temperatures and needn't bother with any lights.

4. Kale

Positive temp: cool to warm. pH: 5.5 - 6.5

Kale is a nutritious and heavenly enhanced plant for home and café dishes. It is an extraordinary vegetable for a sound individual with demonstrated medical advantages. The extraordinary news is that individuals have developed Kale hydroponically for such huge numbers of years, so certainly you can do it in the water framework. Also, indeed, it's anything but difficult to develop and flourish well right now.

5. Cucumbers

Good temp: hot. pH: 5.5 - 6.0

Cucumbers are a typical vining plant that is developed at home and in the business gardens. They appreciate a fast development under adequate condition and consequently give significant returns. There are a few kinds and sizes of cucumbers, including the tough American slicers, long touchy seedless European, and the smooth-cleaned Lebanese cucumbers. All can develop well in Hydroponics. Cucumber is a warm plant so make certain to supply it with enough light and temperature.

6. Spinaches

Good temp: cool to warm. pH: 6.0 - 7.0

Spinach leaves

The most loved vegetable that can be either eaten crude or prepared in your supper grows well in the water-based condition. Spinach is a cool plant, so it doesn't require an excess of light. You can gather it at the same time or remove a few leaves. You can find a workable pace a long time of constant reaping under a decent state of atmosphere and developing condition.

7. Beans

Good temp: warm. pH: 6.0

Hydroponic green beans

One of the most profitable and low-support vegetables that can be developed hydroponically. You can pick the sorts of beans you can develop, including green beans, shaft beans, pinto beans, lima beans. You will require a trellis or something to help the plants if you plant post beans. Seed germination generally takes 3 - 8 days. Gathering starts following 6 - two months. From that point forward, you can proceed with the harvest for 3 - 4 months.

Fruits

8. Strawberries

Great temp: warm. pH: 6.0

Hydroponic strawberries

Strawberries are appropriate for hydroponic developing. Truth be told, these Fruits are one the most famous plants developed in business hydroponic creation. They have been developed in enormous scope NFT frameworks by the business ranches for a considerable length of time. Be that as it may, you can in any case appreciate scrumptious crisp strawberries to take care of all your family by developing them at home and reaping the Fruits throughout the entire year.

9. Blueberries

Good temp: warm. pH: 4.5 - 6.0

Blueberries

Blueberries, an extraordinary organic product high in nutrients for your feast, can be developed well in Hydroponics. This plant takes more time to tolerate organic products than strawberries, frequently until the subsequent years. They are generally developed in a NFT framework. It's difficult to plant blueberries from seeds, so transplants are suggested.

10. Peppers

Great temp: warm to hot. pH: 5.5 - 6.0

Hydroponic sweet peppers

Peppers need the equivalent hydroponic developing condition like tomatoes - warm temperature and a lot of lights. Peppers frequently take a few months to develop

You can either begin developing them from seeds or plants from the neighborhood garden provider. Prescribed assortments for hydroponically developing are Jalapeno, Habanero for hot peppers; Mazurka, Cubico, Nairobi, Fellini for sweet peppers.

Chapter Eight: How To Grow Plants In Easy Way With Hydroponics Practical Guide On

Amount Of Water/Types

Two elements can influence water's capacity to convey broke up Nutrients to your plants: the degree of mineral salts in the water, as estimated by PPM, and the pH of the water. Hard water that contains a high mineral substance won't break up Nutrients as adequately as water with a lower mineral substance, so you may need to channel your water on the off chance that it is high in mineral substance. The perfect pH level for water utilized in a hydroponic framework is somewhere in the range of 5.8 and 6.2 (somewhat acidic). If your water doesn't meet this level, synthetic substances can be utilized to modify the pH into the perfect range.

Amount Of Fertilizer

The Nutrients (or fertilizers) utilized in hydroponic frameworks are accessible in both fluid and dry structures, just as both natural and engineered. Either type can be put into water to make the supplement mix needed by the hydroponic system. The thing you use ought to incorporate both the primary macronutrients—magnesium, phosphorus, nitrogen, potassium, and calcium—just as the significant micronutrients, which incorporate follow measures of iron, manganese, boron, zinc, copper, molybdenum, and chlorine.

Use fertilizers that are intended for hydroponic planting; you ought to have great outcomes If you use them as per bundle headings. Abstain from utilizing standard nursery manures in a hydroponic framework, as their equations are intended for use in garden soil.

Pick hydroponic supplement items intended for your particular needs. For instance, some are advertised as being most appropriate for blossoming plants, while others are best for advancing vegetative development, as verdant greens.

Water Recycling Requirements

Two elements can influence water's capacity to convey disintegrated supplements to your plants: the degree of mineral salts in the water, as estimated by PPM, and pH of the water. Hard water which has a high mineral substance won't disintegrate supplements as viably as water with a lower mineral substance, so you may need to channel your water If it is high in mineral substance. The perfect pH level for water utilized in a hydroponic framework is somewhere in the range of 5.8 and 6.2 (marginally acidic). On the off chance that your water doesn't meet this level, synthetic substances can be utilized to change the pH into the perfect range.

Light Requirements

Hydroponic frameworks are regularly indoor frameworks situated in places where there isn't access to coordinate daylight all through the day. Most consumable plants require six hours of daylight daily; 12 to 16 hours is far superior. Except if you have a sunroom or another space with bunches of window introduction, you'll likely need to give supplemental develop lights. Hydroponic framework packs normally accompany the vital light apparatuses, yet If you are sorting out your own segments, you should buy separate lighting installations.

The ideal lighting for a hydroponics system is HID (High-Intensity Discharge) light apparatuses, which can incorporate either HPS (High-Pressure Sodium) or MH (Metal Halide) bulbs. The light from HPS bulbs discharges a progressively orange-red light, which is incredible for plants in the vegetative development arrange.

T5 is another sort of lighting used in hydroponic develop rooms. It produces a high-yield bright light with low warmth and low energy use. It is ideal for developing plant cuttings and plants with short development cycles.

Make a point to put your lighting framework on a clock so the lights turn on and off simultaneously every day.

Chapter Nine: Pest Control Tips And Tricks

Hydroponics can have some effect on bug pressure yet the greater factor on bug pressure is condition. Hydroponic frameworks are frequently utilized in controlled situations like nurseries or inside. Developing in a controlled domain gives the plant specialist the possibility to totally prohibit bothers from the harvest; yet accomplishing this can be troublesome. By and large, there are a few irritations that get into the nursery and once they get in they can rapidly duplicate. A controlled domain garden is incredible for the two plants and bugs. At the point when a bug gets into an indoor nursery it winds up in a domain with immaculate climate and no predators . . . essentially bug paradise. There are a few strategies for controlling irritations, however frequently the best resistance is avoidance. A large portion of the techniques for bug the board can be utilized in a controlled situation or outside.

Preventive Methods

Preventive strategies incorporate bug avoidance systems like positive weight develop rooms and HEPA consumption channels, depicted prior in the Equipment for Growing Indoors segment. Another rejection practice is wearing clean garments before going into an indoor develop space to abstain from conveying in bugs from outside. Preventive strategies likewise incorporate choosing plant assortments that are fitting for the developing condition and have illness opposition, and giving these plants the water and supplements they should be sufficiently solid to oppose infections.

Physical If preventive practices don't keep bothers out and a bug is found in the nursery, physical bug the executives rehearses are an extraordinary, nontoxic technique for controlling irritations. My preferred physical vermin the executives method is utilizing a vacuum to expel any bugs I spot. Extra physical vermin the executives systems are expelling whole plants and utilizing clingy traps. Clingy traps are likewise utilized for observing irritation levels.

Natural Biological irritation the executives includes the utilization of predators, parasites, and infections to control bother populaces. One of the most well-known organic irritation the board systems for plant specialists is the arrival of ladybugs. Organic nuisance the board may not totally destroy a bug populace, however it for the most part can hold the bug populace in line.

Natural Pesticides Organic pesticides are commonly viewed as less poisonous than regular/manufactured pesticides, however they despite everything ought to be utilized carefully. Continuously check the name on pesticides, even natural ones, to see whether there is any prescribed individual assurance hardware like gloves, goggles, or a respirator. Most ranches can totally oversee bugs utilizing just natural pesticides.

Ordinary Pesticides Conventional, or engineered, pesticides are once in a while required by home plant specialists. Indeed, even business cultivates that are not confirmed natural will regularly exclusively utilize natural pesticides since they are exceptionally compelling. A large portion of the regular pesticides accessible to plant specialists are similarly as protected as natural pesticides when utilized appropriately.

Chapter Ten: Beginners Mistake

Individuals enter the universe of hydroponics for various reasons, these can be for no particular reason or benefit, and in the two roads, it will pay to recognize what you are doing before you make any type of speculation. Like any type of cultivating, the more you do, the more educated you become and the better you are at knowing the prerequisites and complexities of developing plants in a soilless situation.

It takes a rich measure of arranging and research when beginning, and thusly, you can save money on making a few normal, tedious and expensive Mistakes. These are shockingly made again and again by new producers.

Here we will investigate the best 8 Mistakes made by hydroponic producers, and ideally, you can utilize this data to abstain from committing similar Mistakes in your hydroponic endeavor.

For what reason do we center on hydroponic Mistakes and disappointments?

There is a will to absorb information when first beginning in hydroponics, and it is a bend numerous people may attempt to take alternate ways or surge, as opposed to taking as much time as necessary and accurately getting things done. We center on these basic Mistakes in light of the fact that as people, we gain more from blunders and disappointments than we do if something is running effectively.

We can likewise take these Mistakes and use them as chances to learn and improve our hydroponic frameworks, from the main beginnings to scaling up tasks. There will even now be hiccups along, however realizing what the most well-known regions for disappointment and Mistakes, go far to making your hydroponic endeavor a triumph.

Mistake 1: Grow Space and Difficult to Use Systems

Even though a hydroponic framework can be set up in practically any area, this is no motivation to think any space is reasonable. This is one thing which gets numerous producers out on the grounds that they plan frameworks which become hard to oversee.

At the point when a framework isn't planned in light of the developing space, things like work process and proficiency are regularly overlooked. This prompts developing zones that:

- Use space insufficiently
- Are hard to collect
- Can require heaps of tending to and transplanting

- Are not perfect for bother control
- Access to indispensable parts is troublesome

These can differ If you are developing inside or using a nursery. Be that as it may, all factors need considering before you fabricate your framework. This can fall into two classes, developing needs being one, and client needs being the second.

Growing needs

- Developing needs
- Lighting
- Watering
- Supplements
- Are not ideal for pest control
- Warming and stickiness

Client needs

- Access
- Accommodation
- Mechanization
- Excess

A prime model being producers who structure frameworks in a cellar. They have their supplement repository sat along the edge of their develop table, and with regards to the hour of flushing a framework, they have no methods for depleting their store without the utilization of a container.

Mistake: Underestimating System Build Costs

For home producers, a hydroponic framework can be worked for as meager or as much as you need to spend on it. Disparaging these costs paying little heed to framework size can keep producers separate from spending plan, and with a framework, they can't utilize.

Diverse framework types do cost shifting measures of venture. A few frameworks can even be worked without the requirement for buying certain creation things and utilizing items from nearby tool shops. Develop towers and NFT frameworks being genuine models.

Following on from botch #1, it is smarter to completely plan your framework and figure costs before you being establishment.

Mistake: Choosing the Wrong Crops

Figuring each harvest will develop the equivalent in each sort of hydroponic framework is one speedy approach to disappointment. Not exclusively do all plants have various requirements, however some additionally are not appropriate for explicit situations. Developing inside, or outside in a nursery or other developing space will have a particular bearing on this, be that as it may, there are three speedy inquiries to pose to yourself before buying any seeds to develop in your frameworks:

- Are you confronting any atmosphere imperatives?
- What are your developing systems?
- Would you be able to develop the ideal harvests with your creation procedures?

All harvests accompany totally different requirements. There are short and tall plants, and all these must be refined with a specific goal in mind. If you are utilizing a pontoon framework, at that point there is no utilization in hoping to develop tomatoes for instance.

Atmosphere is additionally one constraining element. If you are engaging against high warmth, at that point you have minimal possibility of developing cool climate harvests, and the other way around. Except if you can control temperatures reasonably, there is little motivation to endeavor developing harvests that stand a decent possibility of flopping before you start.

Mistake: Ignoring PH Levels

The initial three Mistakes would all be able to be credited to setting up a framework before really developing. Presently we are at the phase where plants are in danger when things turn out badly. This is one of the most critical regions of any hydroponic framework, and it happens to be one territory which is frequently disregarded or bungled.

This Mistake comes from producers needing to get results as quick as they can and stir up supplements and start watering their plants. The inclination for results keeps cultivators from considering all the recipes and abbreviations they have to know, and the impacts of what accompanies them.

Thinking about PPM, pH, 18/6 and others can be overpowering, however they do assume a significant job. A large number of these terms can be to some degree overlooked, yet pH certainly can't at any expense. At the point when pH levels are out of parity, the plants will endure, and they can endure quicker than numerous producers completely comprehend.

pH decides when supplement arrangements or plain water are acidic or soluble. Customary faucet water has a pH level which much of the time is reasonable for use in hydroponic frameworks. Developing media as a rule is as of now pH adjusted, in spite of the fact that something, for example, Rockwool is more basic than other developing media, for example, coco coir.

pH impartial is a degree of 7.0, which is the thing that most soil developed plants like. In hydroponics, you will in general discover plants incline toward a little underneath this level and have a scope of 5.5 to 6.5 contingent upon the plants being referred to. Numerous supplement insufficiencies originate from pH issues, so ensuring these are under wraps is essential. You can be pursuing issues in different regions, and picking up no ground in tackling them in light of the fact that your pH isn't right.

Both a pH testing unit and furthermore pH altering mixes are fitting, so you can rapidly adjust your supplement blend to the right level (keep an eye every day). When you do as such, your plants can take up all the supplements they need.

Mistake: Using Too Many Nutrients or the Wrong Nutrients

Not all composts are the equivalent. For one thing, customary manure won't break down completely and can rapidly square siphons and channels. Moreover, they don't contain indistinguishable supplements from a decent quality hydroponic equation.

With the right supplement arrangements close by, you at that point need to ensure your blends are at the correct levels. The expansion of such a large number of supplements is excessively simple, and it is a mix-up countless producers clear a path time and again.

A great deal of this issue isn't generally the deficiency of the producer, a portion of the fault is down to the organization providing the supplements. These supplement organizations frequently incorporate taking care of timetables with their items. Sadly, these taking care of timetable measurements are set excessively high.

This rapidly prompts supplement consume (nute consume), and in spite of the fact that it doesn't murder your plants, it will affect how they develop starting now and into the foreseeable future.

To conquer this issue, you can follow a similar taking care of timetable which accompanies your supplements, in any case, slice the measurement to a fourth of what is suggested.

A model being, if the guide is for 2 teaspoons of supplement arrangement per gallon of water, just utilize 1/2 a teaspoon. As a result of doing this, and your pH levels are in extend, you will rapidly check whether there are indications of supplement insufficiency. If so, you can expand the measurements up to half of the prescribed dose per gallon.

Following this strategy, you can likewise eliminate the salt development that happens when your supplement blend is excessively rich.

Mistake: Watering Too Often

The greater part of us were raised to think plants need sun and water each day. At the point when this disposition is combined with cultivators needing to give everything to their plants, they frequently wind up overwatering their plants.

This overwatering can make plants hang, and in outrageous cases, it can make plants experience the ill effects of root decay and pass on. If you can get it in time, you can make changes in accordance with your watering, and plants can reestablish themselves to their full greatness.

The atmosphere or developing condition can influence this, and you should take into account outside temperatures and vanishing. One simple approach to tell If you have your watering plan set accurately is to test the top inch of your developing medium. Utilizing coco coir for instance, if your finger pulls away dry and there is no indication of dampness, at that point the time has come to water your plants.

When utilizing a hydroponic siphon, it will take some experimentation to locate the best equalization, contingent upon your framework.

One thing which is significant is for DWC (profound water culture) frameworks is to ensure you have adequate air stones in your answer. Overwatering is fundamentally a plant being denied of oxygen, so you can have everything set effectively, however without oxygenating your answer, you are as a result overwatering your plants.

Mistake: Not Enough Light

This can be viewed as the second most urgent territory in a hydroponic set-up. Cultivators who don't decide to put effectively in their lighting rig, all the more frequently observe their frameworks fall flat, or possibly they don't convey on the yields they get.

You can undoubtedly represent the deciding moment your hydroponic nursery by overlooking the significance of lighting. Here are three reasons hitting the nail on the head can improve things greatly:

- Purchasing pretty much nothing (little or low force) lighting arrangements, and your plants will endure
- If you buy an inappropriate blubs, at that point your plants won't develop

- If you settle on the least expensive alternatives for your lighting, they probably won't perform

Lighting will be one of the most basic ventures cultivators can make for their frameworks, so it is crucial some examination is completed to see which is the best answer for your developing space, and for the plant types you want to develop.

Fluorescent lighting: Many producers are persuaded these light sorts are reasonable for all plants at all development stages. They are additionally pulled in by their low price.Unfortunately, these sorts of cylinders just emanate a sort of light. White light doesn't convey the full range of light required by plants at the various phases of their development.

Glaring lights are perfect for your seedlings, however once these enter vegetative and blooming stages, they need the entirety of the blue, red and orange pieces of the range.

Shrouded Lamps: these are among the top decision by numerous genuine cultivators. They likewise come in two assortments HPS (High-Pressure Sodium) and MH (Metal Halide) and are regularly observed lighting enormous zones, for example, roads or parking areas.

Although greater, they are in reality more effective than ordinary lights. These bulbs likewise accompany a mechanical or electronic stabilizer that has the capacity of beginning and keeping up the circular segment in the light. These lights do deliver loads of warmth and are frequently found inside ventilation chambers.

A decent dependable guideline is to balance your lights around two feet from the highest point of your plants, and to discover if this is perfect, put your hand on the highest point of your plants and perceive how hot your hand is. If it is unreasonably hot for you, at that point it is unreasonably hot for your plants.

LED Lights: These are new to the universe of hydroponic lighting. Being energy effective, they are fueled by an outside force supply. This force supply much of the time flops before any of the LED develop lights do, yet it very well may be immediately supplanted.

LED's produce less warmth and convey a novel light range that is helpful for photosynthesis.

Picking the correct lighting

When taking a gander at your lighting choices, there are a couple of elements which need taking a gander at. These incorporate spending plan, fenced in area type, ventilation, and plant types.

Low spending producers can decide on ordinary fluorescent cylinders (T5 type) while little scope cultivators are more qualified to utilize the fresher minimized fluorescent cylinders. When you have a progressively broad framework, you would then be able to select the HID lighting frameworks, but since of their warmth yield, you have to check ventilation, and furthermore your taking care of times may change.

Ventilation additionally should be away from your develop room, cooling costs will increment, and it will be difficult to control temperatures.

At present, LED's are left for long haul cultivators, however over their lifetime, they will spare a great many dollars in power bills.

Mistake: Sanitation, or Lack of It

One last Mistake numerous producers make is sanitation in their developing territory. Since hydroponic frameworks are a sterile domain, this stretches out to the whole zone, and not just the frameworks plants are developing. Once there is a component of ailment anyplace in a framework, this can immediately spread and influence not only a couple of plants, it will influence every one of them.

Floors ought to be spotless and dry, and all the apparatuses you may utilize ought to be for the sole motivation behind your hydroponic framework or cleaned altogether before use. This is before you even think about the state of your frameworks.

Supplement repositories can have green growth development after some time, so when you flush your framework, these ought to be examined and cleaned as required. The equivalent goes for channeling and develop beds.

There will be salt development from your supplement blend, and this will stick to pots, and your developing medium, and if these are not altogether cleaned, it can irritate issues when you include your next bunch of supplements.

Plant waste can be one of the most significant, and when you see indications of an issue, this plant ought to be expelled as fast as would be prudent, in light of the fact that any ailing plant will pass it onto the others.

Conclusion

It tends to be too simple to even think about saying it is presence of mind to abstain from committing these Mistakes. In any case, this isn't the situation, and regardless of how cautious you are, there are components which creep in you may be ignorant of. All cultivators do commit Mistakes, and much of the time, it isn't through absence of endeavoring.

There are an immense number of factors having an effect on everything in a hydroponic framework to make them run adequately consistently.

Hydroponics doesn't need to be troublesome, however picking up everything can be overpowering while you are first learning. Ideally, you can utilize all the data above to structure and actualize a well-working framework that can bring you long stretches of bliss and packs of sound plants.

CPSIA information can be obtained
at www.ICGtesting.com
Printed in the USA
LVHW060006240421
685423LV00003B/462